Going to Prison a Teenage Boy

Written by:
Antonio Stowes

Cadmus Publishing
www.cadmuspublishing.com

Copyright © 2021 Antonio Stowes

Published by Cadmus Publishing
www.cadmuspublishing.com

ISBN: 978-1-63751-022-3

All rights reserved. Copyright under Berne Copyright Convention, Universal Copyright Convention, and Pan-American Copyright Convention. No part of this book may be reproduced, stored in a retrieval system, or transmitted in any form, or by any means, electronic, mechanical, photocopying, recording or otherwise, without prior permission of the author.

Contents

Introduction 1

A Disadvantage from the Start 2

The Wrong Color for True Justice 5

Out of Sight, Out of Mind 7

Black Lives Really Do Matter! 10

Always Fight for your Freedom 13

Never Stop Educating Yourself 16

Be Who You Want to Be, Not Who They Say You Are 19

Lose the Street Mentality 22

Believe in a Higher Power 25

Don't Take Nothing for Granted 27

Final Chapter/Conclusion 30

Acknowledgements 32

Fatherless Fathers 34

My Hurt and Pain 35

By Antonio Stowes (Buckey Lo) 2019 35

Introduction

My name is Antonio "Buckey Lo" Stowes. I was born February, 7th, 1994 in Cleveland, Ohio, St. Luke's hospital. The struggle has been real for me, right from birth. Being born in the 90's meant a lot of us were, "quote on quote" crack babies. My mother Antonia "Ann" Stowes was battling an addiction to cover up all the hurt and pain she had endured and experienced in the course of her life (She eventually won the battle and has been sober ever since, I'm so proud of her & your life was spared because you could have easily been killed by the hands of Anthony Sowell, like several of your other friends, R.I.P to all the women involved). Another alarming statistic, my father was unknown and very absent and that's a forever ongoing battle and struggle in the black households and communities! If it wasn't for "Henry Rigsby" (1933-2020), known as grandfather, taking me in at the hospital, I would of for sure been lost in the foster care system. Being the only child, I had to walk this crazy journey called life by myself. You can only imagine without the proper support and guidance what my future life would lead too!? The streets, violence, womanizing, let downs, pain, struggle, and the inevitable it seems like "PRISON"! This Cycle has to come to a halt and in my era and generation, I will do much as I can to make a difference. This is my whole mission and purpose of writing a book to speak for so many young black men, who can relate to my upbringing and who also may have so much in common with my upbringing and journey. Please take the time to read this book from cover to cover!

Chapter 1
A Disadvantage from the Start

The year 2020 sparked a fire in me something so fierce! History of blacks being mistreated and targeted, repeated itself but we became fed up after the George Floyd killing, by a police officer.

Like a lot of young African American kids growing up are always naive or oblivious to the unfairness, injustice, or inequality. You think the ghettos and hoods we're growing up in are okay and acceptable. We become a product of our environment and the violence, drugs, death, prison, lack of education and absent strong male black fathers become normal. This really made me feel some type of way.

A black woman judge sentenced me to 18 years, my first adult offense for Aggravated robbery that I committed at the age of 17. The simple fact that I robbed white individuals is my strong belief because I received a for sure disproportionate prison sentence. I appealed my Sentence, it was reversed and remanded back because the courts admitted they "strayed drastically" away from the sentence guidelines. Unfortunately, I was resentenced to the same exact 18-year prison term to "quote on quote", protect the public from future crimes I "could" possibly commit. Needless to say, to my people who may be reading this book "please" don't never lay down or stop fighting the system. Always fight the justice system for your Freedom, whether you're guilty or innocent because it's your freedom and life. Don't ever feel defeated my brother's, period.

A lot of us had it hard from the very start, we weren't fully aware that the journey ahead would be full of so many obstacles, trials, and tribulations! Growing up I was always told; a hard head makes a soft ass and Its hard to get out of them white folks' custody once you're in it. So many other things to grab my attention from a verbal standpoint were said to me often but where was the good examples for me to follow after?? Nonexistent! When with dealing a lot of young African American youth, you have to show them people that they can relate too and have something in common with to grab their attention. I want to be a good example for many people who can relate and to prevent younger generations from going this path at all. It hurts my heart and soul every time, I watch the news or TV and its nothing but senseless violence going on, untimely deaths, and suffering. I just want to make a difference and being in prison, not being able to contribute to bettering things for my family and community, has been very disheartening to say the least.

A lot of other races or people from different cultures, may disagree but blacks are truly treated unfairly in basically every aspect of life. This book is not to complain about the issues blacks have endured for so long but to enlighten my young black brothers and sisters so they can be fully aware of what lies ahead of them. It's very possible to become successful but you have to be prepared and equipped with the right tools, support, and knowledge to defeat the odds.

Having a target on our backs right from the beginning is basically ensuring the odds that failure is "inevitable" for majority of our race. That's why it's very important to educate each other and make it known that we indeed have "alternatives" and "options" for our lives, outside of the norms of our peers, family members and people in our neighborhoods! You should always strive to be better than anybody you know and actually want better results. We put limitations and barriers on our minds consciously and unconsciously that stop us from achieving, pursuing, and accomplishing our dreams, goals, and true aspirations. Sometimes, we may be discouraged but that is just a mere feeling, it is more than possible to achieve the things you manifest and create in your mind!

Chapter 2

The Wrong Color for True Justice

The system is without a doubt unfair. Its already bad enough that so many black men are dying in the communities to the hands of senseless black on black violence, police killings, and unfortunate health issues. Not that the problems aren't enough but the prison system, which was formed to "rehabilitate", correct, and punish us, solely focuses on punishing us.

Statistics are mind blowing and the disproportionate sentences and consequences have been occurring for way too long! I was born in the 90's and growing up I was naive to many things especially the criminal justice system and how it works. A study released by the bureau of justice statistics and the prison policy initiative as of 2019, states that the American criminal justice system holds almost 2.3 million people in 1,719 state prisons, 109 federal prisons, 1,772 juvenile correctional facilities, 3,163 local jails, 80 Indian country jails, many military prisons and immigration detention facilities. All these facilities were made to hold human beings like animals.

More facts that show the mass incarceration and why the recidivism statistics are always up or on the rise. Technical violations are the main reason for incarceration of people on probation or parole. Most of these individuals (98% percent) are " reincarcerated" without committing a new offense. In Ohio majority of offenders face double jeopardy because you're sentenced to 3 to 5 years mandatory of parole, even if you max out or complete your entire prison term or sentence! That's a set up for failure because you're on a short lease with basically no room to breathe. I want my young brothers and sisters who may be reading this book, to be fully aware of how the system is playing us so please make better choices and wise decisions.

Also contrary to myths, people incarcerated for "violent offenses" and released are "least" likely to be arrested again. By almost any measure, people who are released after serving time in prison for violent offenses are the least likely to reoffend. Next are the least likely to be rearrested again for any offense, least likely to be convicted again, least likely to be incarcerated again and least likely to be sentenced to prison again. The system overlooks violent offenders or people who commit violent crimes, time after time. Instead of focusing in on only nonviolent offenders, they need to actually take a serious look at people with serious offenses, who have spent years and years in prison and may actually be rehabilitated.

For my young black brothers, who are having run ins with the law or is starting a cycle of incarceration at a young age, please find or create a better path. I say this because the system will swallow you up very young and not care about your future. A lot of dudes who I either grew up with, went to school with, or played football with have been incarcerated or had to endure some type of probation or parole. Also, more disturbing facts, about the 63,000 youth in confinement in the united states (This number will continue to grow year after year), too many are there for a serious offense that is not even a crime. For example, there are over 8,100 youth behind bars for technical violations of their probation, rather than for a new offense. An additional 2,200 youth are locked up for status offenses, which are behaviors that are not law violations for adults, such as running away, truancy and incorrigibility. Nearly 1 in 10 youth held for a criminal or delinquent offense is locked in an adult jail or prison, and most of the others are held in juvenile facilities that look and operate a lot like prisons and jails. This something that needs to be attacked early on, especially since the youth are our future right!? The value of our youth should be more significant and a lot of black youth deserve better options, alternatives and opportunities!

Chapter 3
Out of Sight, Out of Mind

So many people can relate to me and feel my energy on this chapter title. Some of the worst feelings of been locked up are feeling ignored, irrelevant, and worthless. Its many more feelings to express what's on our minds and hearts daily but I want to explain the depth of " out of sight, out of mind".

A lot of us don't understand the concept of "out of sight - out of mind. It's painful at times to know that people you truly love, are living their lives and you can't be a part of it. Its days that I feel like I don't exist especially when it comes to certain people. No matter your role, you played in the lives of your family or friends before prison, the love and support will not always be returned. What we fail to realize, is that some people don't know how to ride with us or be here for us consistently as we would like or need. Knowing that you still exist but your presence is absent to the free world (A.K.A.) society and you are not receiving the same love and attention as you once were can be mentally draining.

Its certain loved ones that I think about daily but yet I have not spoken to some of them in years. Feeling unloved, will do something internally to you that will either break you down or motivate you. I let it motivate me to never put myself in these circumstances again, mainly because the years I lost to the system could have been years in society, where I could have accomplished many things. Every time I call somebody phone and they ignore my calls or constantly don't answer, that drives me to make it home soon as possible so I can determine who I accept or deny in my life.

The JPay site was created for us to stay in touch with our loved ones and it made communication so much easier and better for us. It's also very cheap and affordable but yet so many decent people incarcerated get no love on them at all. My reason of speaking on JPay is because its "no excuse" why many loved ones of people incarcerated can be all on social media sites, posting pictures and videos all day everyday but can't correspond on a consistent basis using JPay!? In my opinion there is no excuse to have a lack of communication. True love has no limit and shouldn't be circumstantial.

Committing my offense at the age of 17 and being sentenced to 18 years at the age of 18 did something to me psychologically, in a motivational type of way. It was unreal that a child had received all this time for a crime where nobody was harmed physically and my two adult codefendants at the time received 3 years' probation (I was swapped out). Being young and naive, I thought all my friends and family members were going to ride with me, support me and stay in my corner a 100% percent because they simply said they were, well that was not how things played out.

I was a very known person in my neighborhood and in the city of Cleveland, my generation growing up, from a street aspect. I truly was loyal to the streets and the wrong people, which led to me being tricked out of my freedom. When it was all said and done, only a few people remained in my corner. As we all learn over time, (for ones who mothers still are alive), mom dukes are the ones that hold it down, whether you're there or not especially for people that came down as a teenager or young adult. My grandfather held it down until the day he died literally. I was blessed to have a "few" good friends and family members who remained in my life, no matter what was said about me or my character! Instead of us being out of sight, out of mind, let us be out of sight but in the hearts of our loved ones every single day.

Far as the romantic aspect and for my young brothers who have females they love or care about, read carefully. Trying to maintain a steady relationship is hard and difficult while locked up but very possible. You will stress yourself out, trying to keep up and maintain the same consistent, intimate, and normal relationship. For majority of us men incarcerated, we may have a loyal female in our corner but believe it's difficult for her to ride so never take a "good woman" for granted, especially in these circumstances. For the men who have woman who are not standing by your side, please understand every woman is not equipped with the right mentality, devotion, will power, or loyalty to hold you down. Once you understand that, you will be able to focus your time on bettering "yourself", instead of chasing a ghost. Moving forward, if you truly love your woman make better decisions so you can stay free for her in the physical form. Furthermore, we must make better choices so we can stop being absent in the lives of our loved one's period. They need us more then we can imagine and even though they need us and miss us, doesn't mean they will stop living their lives for us. Another disappointing fact is people will jump in and out of your life so often that it will be something you become accustomed too. You will have consistent communication and correspondence with a person, then it will be you wondering why this person is not responding back or no longer communicating with you. That is always a hard pill to swallow and if you did that to a loved one in society, it could potentially become a problem.

Next, please stop glorifying coming to prison, thinking that you're solid or a stand-up person because you donated and forfeited, precious time out of your life for dumb decisions or stupidity. People will post you all on their social media profiles, saying "free you " but won't support you financially consistently, or emotionally by checking up on you to see if you're still mentally sane or stable. "Stop tricking", yourself out of your freedom simple as that!

Chapter 4
Black Lives Really Do Matter!

After the 2020 killing of George Floyd, the "entire" world finally paid attention to how black people have been suffering for so long. After the murder of George Floyd, it has become a trend to scream # Black lives matter and this is bigger than a movement, this is a lifestyle for us black folks. While the Corona Virus was in full force, "our true pandemic" is the deaths and murders of black people at rapid paces in America! It seems like anything that has to do with fatality, we are always highly affected by it. As I grow older this disturbs me more and more.

The length of our natural lives is already shorter then basically every other race but most of us don't even make it to see our 30's alive or as a free man in society due to senseless violence. We know its difficult circumstances in our neighborhoods and so often we become products of our environment, which is so unfortunate. It's so many targets on our backs dealing with racism but yet it seems like we are "our own" worst enemies. My entire life so far, black on black homicides have been an issue that has been so difficult to find a solution for. It's been so difficult over the course of my incarceration to constantly watch on the news, day after day, our own take each other's lives especially the youth of our communities. I must use my voice because it's ridiculous that we lose our lives to the ignorant people in society or to the prison system.

I sit back every day and analyze how many of these dudes that

are incarcerated with me actually value life. For most people in life, once you have experienced a traumatic situation it usually makes you view life and the world in a different light but sadly, some people continue the same behavior patterns or negative routines. It seems like not many dudes around me value their lives, especially the ones who still have a certain mentality for destruction. I see dudes smoke K-2 (tune) all day every day, until they nod out, pass out, or become belligerent. From personal experience, that stuff is so damaging mentally and it destroys good character. These are unknown substances that are being smoked. I understand it's an attempt to escape the hurt and pain of are harsh reality of being incarcerated but that stuff is not for human beings, period! I just want to see us make better decisions moving forward. Another issue that is contradicting is that black lives actually do matter but its legal and okay to deem prisoners slaves, using the 13th amendment. According to the 13th amendment, once you lose your freedom due to committing a crime, you're a slave voluntarily. If it's supposed to be fair, equal, and true justice the 13th amendment should be amended. We are being deceived and tricked so we must educate ourselves more and more every day.

Once you've been living so reckless for so long, it's hard to change your ways and mentality but that is needed if you want to have better results out of your life moving forward. A lot of dudes truly feel it is a waste of time or pointless to start reinventing yourself " while in prison" but this the place where you should want to truly change and rehabilitate "yourself" on your own because without you actually applying yourself, you will not change, or you can become worse. I feel if you honestly prep, groom and prepare yourself to reenter society, you will have some type of success.

I had an immature and purposeless type of thinking, mentality, and demeanor for so long but I felt I was wasting time and I felt like my life was meaningless. Even though, I'm incarcerated I wanted to find my true purpose and have something to work towards. When I started thinking different, meaning I stopped associating with dudes who didn't have the same vision or mind frame as me. As a result, it was so much negativity sent my way and all type of lies and false rumors were said about me and my character. That's sad, it's no way that anyone could or should be mad that I truly wanted to change my life for the better. We should always embrace and acknowledge, when somebody is making the effort to start valuing their one life, not spit venom or negativity!

The unity amongst us African Americans is so shaky and we need to come together, stand behind each other and stop harming each other period! It seems like the only time we come together is when someone is actually murdered, will be at a vigil, memorial or funeral. The gathering or sense of unity will only last temporary, then back to the madness. It will be so lovely and magnificent for "us all" to unite for the better cause permanently! I remember first coming to prison as an 18-year-old teenager, that was a feeling that seemed all too normal to the "Odrc" (Ohio Department of Rehabilitation and Corrections) And I'm sure all around the country. It was many people who I came across that were shocked to see me in prison, doing 18 at 18, my first adult offense and nobody was harmed physically!? Well, it's not okay or normal to imprison us at such a young age and not give us fair prison sentences. I should have been preparing for prom, college, sports, a girlfriend but I was waiting on a clothes box and worrying about what was for chow.

I wasn't no angel or saint growing up but I wasn't the worst kid by far in society. If it wasn't for me wanting to evolve and elevate, I would of for sure got loss in the system with an institutionalized or prison mentality, like many men around me unfortunately. It's so many of us intelligent, talented, skilled, and bright black men incarcerated but most will never overcome the street or prison mentality. The way most of us are treated, shows that our lives are not valued as much as the next race so the least we can do ourselves is to move a certain way with our actions "showing" that we care about our lives!

Chapter 5
Always Fight for your Freedom

Feeling defeated, is a feeling a lot of us have felt, due to being incarcerated. When you lose trial or plead guilty, it seems like your whole world has collapsed and it's no way to come back from that. That feeling is even worse when you receive a lengthy prison term. Well, I heard the best advice, from a guy named "Darrell Houston" at a black entrepreneur expo in Richland Correctional. What he said stuck with me so I must pass that advice on. " He said no matter if you're guilty or not, always fight for your freedom because ITS YOUR!" That is such a fact so to all my incarcerated people please don't never lay it down and accept some time another human being gave you!

In the beginning of my prison bid, I was terrible and I was involved in all type of nonsense. I was indulging myself in pointless gang activity because that was the cool or popular thing to do. I never became to obsessed, addicted, or infatuated with that lifestyle though. Regardless of what was going on, I remained in the law library consistently. Taking back my freedom was and still is my main priority. It's so many distractions in prison and the average person will lose sight of the main objective, go home soon as possible!

Early on in my prison bid, I had my issues like any other teenager would but I managed to always make time to understand my case, sentence and situation better. Unfortunately, I couldn't afford a lawyer to fight my appeal so I had to do it pro-se (Thanks to the twins Gary & Greg Walker). I had no knowledge of the law, which is the case with majority of young black men coming through the prison/justice system. The goal is to seek out help from legit jail house lawyers, law library clerks, or individuals who have a fair amount of knowledge about the law. Along the way, soak up much as you can and learn as much as you can so you will no longer be ignorant to the law.

You would think no matter who the person is or how old they are, if we are in prison the main focus, goal, and narrative should be getting released soon as possible. The honest truth is most conversations revolve around irrelevant things, that cannot help you get your freedom back. I have been in several different prisons and for individuals my age group or generation, the mentality was the same. What I mean is that very few of us were truly and consistently focused on obtaining our freedom back, whether it was by appeal, judicial release, post-conviction, or clemency. I first hand know it's difficult to get things over turned or reversed but you must fight regardless. The court system is use to people just laying down and not fighting a hard-fought legal battle. This is due to the lack of criminal knowledge, financial stability, and resources that aren't available. Once you understand this, you will know how to prepare yourself to go to war with the system in a proper legal manner.

The thing that the system doesn't believe in and it's shown in the outrageous sentences that are handed out, over and over again. It doesn't believe we can truly change for the better. I can personally say that after being in prison for an X amount of time, your thoughts, mentality, and demeanor will begin to change after you realized that you're losing years and years out your life that you can't get back and that this environment is toxic. I understand its harsh sentencing laws in place, especially mandatory gun specifications that must be served consecutive, to any other existing charge in the state of Ohio. Many judges abuse their discretion and emotionally, or morally sentence us unfairly. Even when there is obvious misconduct, corruption and wrong doing involved in a case, the court system on different levels will still uphold, overrule, or affirm these decisions and sentences. That alone, will knock the spirit out of any of us and make us want to give up! If you feel like the system cannot lose, it will knock you off your square but you must remain in strong spirits!

Its many days and nights that it's hard for me to see the light at the end of the tunnel and I have an actual outdate to be released. I just can imagine how many other individuals who have to see the parole board feel because their immediate freedom is in the hands of people who honestly don't want to see you free! I have met some of the most intelligent men ever in prison, who are also some very strong wielded men but I have seen them at their lowest and breaking point. When being imprisoned is depriving you of your true manhood or fatherhood that can be the effect. With that being said, I've seen them still continue to push forward and constantly stay in the law library faithfully, as opposed to wasting precious time focusing on things that don't matter. I understand we do time Indulging in things that will make our time go faster, or smoother but I feel as if these things distract us. I want all our minds to forever remain focused on freedom on every level.

In the state of Ohio there are many traps to assist us in becoming reincarcerated so once we physically gain our freedom back, we must continue to have the same mindset that helped us gain our freedom back. Even though you were released from behind these gates, walls, and doors don't stop fighting for complete "Freedom". Do your best to be released off of any probation or parole soon as possible. Another thing is always reach back once you've been released and help others who are still incarcerated get on the path to regain their freedom as well. A lot of dudes go home and forget about the struggle and the people in it and that is not stand up at all. Everyone will need that push, motivation, drive, talk, or conversation from you to help them kick start their pursuit of freedom! Please keep your focus on obtaining, securing and keeping your freedom because it's yours!

Chapter 6
Never Stop Educating Yourself

As you grow older you learn how important education and knowledge is. In most situations, the more knowledge you have the more opportunities will become available to you. Growing up, I didn't take education as serious as I should have. My younger years I loved school but as I started getting older, my mind lost interest and desired other things. Even just with the typical school subjects, it was still a lot of things we weren't learning, such as our true history and black history. This is not taught in school class rooms and that's hindering a lot of us.

It's unbelievable what was going on during the corona virus madness. So many schools were afraid to continue in class education and having that in class experience is needed for social and development purposes. Doing virtual classes will be difficult. Just knowing all kids will struggle in some way, which is very unfortunate but minority children will really suffer. This of course will lead to so many issues that will have negative results more than likely. We all just hoped post pandemic that education and learning would go back too normal.

The prison system was indeed hindered by the corona virus. This is the place where the main objective is rehabilitation. When the virus hit it set us back because all of our earned credits or good days are achieved through the education department. For instance, I'm enrolled in college at Ashland University and many different outside professors were allowed to enter the prison too teach the courses. That was so good and refreshing for us guys incarcerated because it gave us a feeling of normalcy and made us feel like a true human being. It made the learning process much simpler and easier to understand. Now we must do everything on the tablets, which is somewhat difficult because we can't ask the on-spot questions or get help when needed. Regardless, I'm determined to learn more about many different things and nothing or nobody will stop me from doing so.

    The more you learn, the more you become conscious of so many new things that can open your mind and world up. At one point of time the Ohio prisons had a time frame or requirement you had to have in order to attend college. You had to have five years or less, to be released or going in front of the parole board which was so unfair. That is basically still in place for the trades or vocational school and that shouldn't be like that. It should be an equal opportunity for everyone in these circumstances to be eligible for every educational program, no matter your prison sentence. Also honestly speaking, many individuals who are doing short prison terms don't care about furthering their education, which is unfortunate because its "free" while in prison. I see men around me of all ages every single day, neglect the opportunity to take advantage of the very few things that can have a positive impact on their future. It's a shame because this is the place where you should reinvent, rebuild, learn more, and actually rehabilitate yourself. Once you start to become conscious of more and more things your mind, perception, and vision will begin to expand as well, and you will desire better results. It's pointless to do your time not learning nothing and sitting around doing your time and simply just that is not going to cut it. You should always be hungry for more knowledge, especially things that you can use to your advantage upon release in society.

    I was so anxious and eager to attend college because I wanted my prison bid to be more of a blessing in disguise, instead of a punishment. Every chance I get, I'm yearning to learn more and strengthening my mental so I can be fully equipped for society. As you seek out more education and gain better, clearer insight on things that were once confusing you will eventually want more and more. The more you obtain, your thoughts will become more fruitful and fluent. That's why I seek out more knowledge in almost every situation behind these walls. In prison, you tend to isolate yourself from dealing with certain individuals, which could stop you from learning much more. The odd thing is you can learn different skills, crafts or knowledge from the most insane, crazy, weird, or odd person. I have met men in here who are loners basically or antisocial but they were some of the brightest men mentally. I gained so much insight from building with these guys that I will always remember. I turned my prison sentence into an all-around learning lesson and humbling experience so I can honestly be rehabilitated and restored as a human being. I refuse to go home without elevating my mind and soaking up much as I can so I can thrive in the free world!

Chapter 7

Be Who You Want to Be, Not Who They Say You Are

I am a firm believer that if you constantly hear people say that you are something or destined to be something, then you will start believing them. Usually, that is said in a negative manner. It's very possible for young black boys and girls to become anything they choose. Sometimes we fall victim to the typical or normal things that we see going on around us. Like for instance, in our black communities, for protection purposes, we may start carrying guns at a very young age. Eventually, we may actually have to use the gun because our life may truly be in danger at some point so we should have more than a right to honestly defend ourselves. The mentality is so toxic in our neighborhoods it's unreal at times. Once you are known for carrying or shooting a gun, then you're labeled a shooter. This was an ignorant label that was given to me and that label comes with so much. This made the police harass or accuse me of doing things that I honestly had no involvement in, this made people fear me and think so negative of me. That is not what I wanted to deal with as a teenager but my older guys from my hood didn't show us a better way.

I wanted to be a football player, teacher, mentor, businessman, father or just a normal person but without the proper support and firm guidance, my dreams were shattered at a young age. So many people were saying you're not going to be this and you're not going to be that and that shot my self-esteem. It was some of my everyday friends who had both a mom, dad, and a better situation. These same guys talked bad, negative, degrading and nasty about me, even though I was one of the most loyalist friend to them. I'm explaining this because if your homies or close friends don't encourage you to strive for more or support you that can make you start to believe that you may really never amount to nothing, even though I know I deserved better because I know that I'm a good person and it is more to my true character then what society is projecting. A lot of us young black kids were bright but all our gifts, skills, talents or true character was overshadowed by the mistakes we made or the non-supportive people around us.

Now in this prison setting, people tend to be followers and are easily influenced. You have so many men portraying to be somebody they're not, basically to fit in. This leads to guys not taking the proper steps or effort to find themselves or their true purpose. Instead of you striving to be down, accepted, or liked, you should strive to be yourself, or imitate someone that is worthy of being followed. Usually, the type of characters you're around, will be the type of character you are or will eventually become. Once I started isolating myself or separating myself from the certain crowd or individuals, I was once associated with I felt freer, determined, and purpose driven. As I started dealing with the right type of men around me, mostly older guys who have been through the same phases I am going through, it made me tap into my true purpose and potential. Dealing with guys who still glorified the streets, violence, nonsense, and ignorance would not help me evolve at all. Being around the right people in prison will help you become better or tap into your true you. When I hear the saying, dare to be different, that should be said or used more often, when you're around or associated with negative, bitter, miserable, lazy, or unambitious people.

A lot of times in life, certain things that work for you may not work as well for the next person so please don't force your way of living or lifestyle on someone else. In this environment for instance, its many dudes who try to bid like other guys they rock with or hang out with. For some individual's things seem to always be stressful or drama filled so why would you want to move or bid like that. Just because they smoke, stay up all day, all night, and are always looking to get into physical alterations, doesn't mean that's the way you should conduct yourself. Unfortunately, its many dudes who are serving lengthy prison sentences and don't understand the importance of starting your prison bid off smooth, simple and focused on your appeal, rehabilitating yourself, and just making things easy as possible for you and your loved ones.

    Early on in my bid I was leading and following the stupid trend of being careless, reckless, violent, and ignorant because this is what everybody I was associated with was doing. Instead of finding a better way to conduct myself, I faced consequences often. This led to me being transferred from prison to prison. My security level started off as a level 2 and in less than two years, I was a level 4 sitting in Lucasville (Which Is a maximum-security prison In Ohio). Having to constantly face these consequences of going to the hole and losing the limited privileges I had took a toll on me, my mother, and grandfather, the ones who stood in my corner every step of the way. It's a crazy feeling to already be in prison but to get cuffed up in handcuffs, time after time again just to be escorted to the hole is humiliating. I wanted to teach and train myself how to avoid unnecessary confrontations and hole shots because if I couldn't stay trouble free or drama free in here, how will I do it in society!? Now its certain Corrections Officers or staff that will provoke certain situations but most of the time you can dodge them individuals. Basically, going to the hole over and over wasn't my thing and I always cared whether I went to the hole.

    In prison it's very important to find or create your lane because it will surely determine if you grow or stay stagnant! Once again, if you're reading this book please soak up what I'm saying so if you're in the beginning or middle of your bid, please make wise decisions on how you will do your time.

Chapter 8
Lose the Street Mentality

So many of us black men, have fallen victim to the Illusion of the streets, a reputation, or politics of it. It's always been understood that if you're in the streets, then you must abide by certain rules or codes. These rules or codes are a set up for failure and play a major part in why so many of us are locked away or prematurely dead. There is no one to truly enforce the rules so obviously many plays unfair.

I am informing you now that no matter how smart, slick, or smooth you think you are, there is still a possibility that you may end up in prison or worse dead. It bothers me to know that so many of us have tricked ourselves out of our freedom and spots in society. By doing so we are tearing our families apart when we decide to remain loyal to the nonsense in the streets or individuals that don't have your best interest at heart. For instance, its so many men who didn't tell or snitch on someone that may have actually committed the crime you may be incarcerated for and this someone may be a good friend to you but they don't hold it down like they should after you are serving time for them. You're willing to miss out on your whole life but that person you took the fall for isn't your biggest supporter while you do your bid. Be mindful who you consider a friend.

Being in the streets or being heavily associated with it, you know violence is so normal or common. Things should not be this way in are communities or neighborhoods. Eventually it becomes boring and foolish after you truly understand that its worthless and pointless to live that way. Also, once you evolve, you learn that human energy is better expended on creation than destruction. Senseless violence is a prerogative of youth, which has much energy but little talent for the constructive. Our youth need to be focusing on more productive things, instead of building street cred, which holds no merit.

When I was running the streets and my name was starting to become very known and popular in Cleveland, Ohio, I thought that was cool and everything at that point in my life. What I did not know was that, I was building a resume that would surely get me hired into prison. Me getting in trouble as a juvenile was me starting the life of a "career criminal", according to the justice system so that was justification to give me an 18-year prison sentence for aggravated robbery my first adult offense but my codefendants received 3 years' probation. Like everything I was doing in the streets did nothing but harm me. For the people who may be fully involved with the streets or may be incarcerated at the moment but still may consider going back to the streets once you're released, please evaluate everything and make wise choices and decisions. The goal is to remain free, build your legacy, create generational wealth, travel, create many good memories, cherish family, and outshine any labels or stereotypes. If you're incarcerated or if you die at early premature age, then you allowed the streets to trick you out your spot. When you move with a street mentality, you will be self-defeated because that way of living will eventually bring you down.

For any young man, who came into the system as a teenager or young adult, please adopt a new mentality that can allow you to be productive, progressive, and prosperous. I want to be able to be there for my loved ones every step of the way and vice versa so in order to make that happen, you must think better and wiser every single day.

I'm 26 years old as I write this book and my outlook on many things has changed over time especially since I have been incarcerated since the age of 17. It's still a lot of growing, grooming, and developing to do but I am mentally beyond my years. It's a shame but the average male this particular age may still be chasing or focused on nonsense that cannot be helpful to your future. I tend to build and communicate with older guys who can truly understand me. Now don't get me wrong, I rock with guys my age as well but if you're not looking to better yourself, gain wisdom, or have meaningful conversations, then I will limit my interaction with individuals who don't want to take the time to reinvent themselves.

I have learned so much over the course of these years and sitting on the bench of life for so long, has made me eager to become a starter in life permanently. I don't want to be the same persona leaving prison and neither should you. I desire to be wiser, better, stronger, smarter, patient, and prepared. Holding on to the same mentality or demeanor will hinder you from getting ahead. I just encourage to put your heart and mind in a better place and strive for greatness!

Chapter 9
Believe in a Higher Power

It's a lot of things that happen in our lives that we can't understand, simple as that. One thing I know is that we have a creator and that person is "God" regardless of the one you believe in. Being spiritual and believing in some type of God will keep you grounded and create some type of moral structure in your life. With that being said you shouldn't frown upon someone else's beliefs because you feel that your way of living or beliefs are better.

I grew up basically only knowing, learning, and believing in Christianity but yet it was so many other religions out there. What's so odd is that the man who raised me, Henry Rigsby, he was Muslim but he never forced that way of living on me. He still embraced Jesus Christ and even Jehovah Witness. I respect him for still allowing me to acknowledge whatever I felt free too. For instance, I love and respect my late uncle Dwight "Choker" Stowes, my aunt cookie (His wife), and big older cousin Shanita Stowes-Brown. They are devoted Christians and God-fearing people and they were long time members of the Word church in Cleveland, Ohio. My uncle was a personal bodyguard to Dr. R.A. Vernon. My only issue was I felt like if I didn't worship the lord or believe everything that the Bible said, then I wouldn't be good enough or accepted by them a 100%. That made me feel inadequate or like I wasn't living up to their standards. That is never healthy for young men or women growing up. You should always allow your children to explore other religions and beliefs and love them regardless of their decisions.

Everybody has to have hope and faith in something or their lives will seem purposeless or undirected. Just imagine coming to prison at such a young age and tender point in your life, you don't know what to believe in or you don't know who you are as a person? As I grew mentally more and more and connected with the right type of men around me, I started learning so much about different beliefs and religions. This opened my eyes to things that I had no knowledge of and may have never became aware of it, if it wasn't for coming to prison. I just want everybody to stand for something or you'll truly fall for anything. If you go through your life not having solid beliefs, you may tend to follow anything or anybody. I don't look down on nobody else's way of life or living. Also, just because someone else has a point of view or perspective on life, doesn't mean that they are less of a person then you or inferior to you. Always remain open to learning about others and their beliefs.

In society or in my current environment (Prison), you need things to help keep you sane or mentally focused and being spiritual or religious will allow that. It will also allow you to have better understanding and make sense of many different things that will transpire in the course of your life. Always remember that your actions and will power will determine a lot of your fate or destiny but it's still a lot of things that is determined by our God, creator, the universe, and higher power.

Chapter 10
Don't Take Nothing for Granted

Being incarcerated since I was a minor has made me immensely grateful for the love and support that I have still. It's so many men around me who have no one in the corner so I always count my blessings.

I feel like a lot of individuals nowadays, don't cherish the things or people they should and that's an issue. First, we should all value our lives a lot more and our actions will show that. As I have been sitting in prison for all these years, I have seen so many dudes come and go or lose their lives about insignificant things or situations. The value of black lives is not enough and that narrative needs to change. Secondly, freedom is not cherished enough. It shouldn't be no way if you receive a second chance, you blow it or if you get chance after chance you constantly make unwise choices and decisions. Obviously, your freedom means nothing to you if you can't stay out of prison. I promise I'm around so many men who are eager, desperate, hungry, or thirsty for another chance at freedom. These men will hit the ground running and take care of their business asap with no excuses! We all need to start moving better so we can keep our freedom.

I know things in society are rough or difficult and it's hard to stay positive, grateful, or focused but you must always remember that its people who are doing worst then you, incarcerated, or dead. Let that being on your mind, will allow you to always remain humble and grounded.

It's so many things that you may have took for granted in your life and some will never realize it until it's taken away, lost for good, you die too early in life, you're ignorant, or you become incarcerated. One of the major things that a lot of us men take for granted is fatherhood and being a father in general.

When you're a teenager the last thing you're thinking about is having a child but this becomes reality for some of us. My teenage years were rocky, and I was having run ins with the law, going through the phases of not having a father, or mother consistent enough in my life, and just the many different struggles of growing up in the hood/ghetto. Well unfortunately, about two months before I got locked up, I was informed that I had a child on the way. This was hard to believe because I never had children before and the woman who claimed I was the father of her unborn child, we were not in a relationship prior and we had a one-night stand. I didn't take it seriously so she felt some type of way and the rage, revenge, and spitefulness begun and it is currently still in progress. We did a "DNA" test about 3 months after "Aria Baer" was born and the results came back "99.99%", that she was indeed my biological daughter. This changed my whole outlook on life but it was a little too late because I was already in the beginning of serving an 18-year prison term. I regret not taking her word serious and should have start preparing to be a father, which would have possibly prevented me from coming to prison. My mother, family, and friends did everything they could to be a part of Aria's life consistently but nothing was good enough and eventually all communication was stopped completely. This hurt me and my mother a lot and this is something that eats at me every day. I continue to build myself up every day as well so I can hopefully redeem myself as father. If you have a chance to be a part of your children life in some form or fashion, please cherish that and always show and express your love to them often. I commend all the men who went home after prison and redeemed themselves as a father and any other role that was needed.

We all are not perfect and we all have flaws that exist within us. I say that because we may not become aware of certain things or realize that we have been taking many things for granted, until it's too late or at a certain point in our lives. The things that you do have in your life and claim to value, such as family, freedom, good health, financial stability, a strong faith in understanding your beliefs/religion, or just breath in your body still. Start showing with your actions that indeed you are grateful for something.

Many days and nights, I lay in this steel bunk and think about the things and people that I will be appreciative of this time around. I am very conscious and it's no reason that a conscious person shouldn't make conscious decisions. With that being said, I will do my best to not take things for granted that actually mean something to me and freedom is definitely top on that list.

Final Chapter/Conclusion

This book writing experience has been fun and very expressing and I desire to write more in life.

Now I hope the ones who actually took the time to read this book, truly benefit from it in some positive way. The harsh reality is that in America, its so many young men who will come through the prison system at some point. Now once you're arrested, your growth and development "mentally" is usually slowed or halted completely. Look up the definition of the word "arrest" and see what it says.

This is a big issue because these are the same young men who may be reentering society again. How do you expect us to prosper out there in a fast-moving world as an adult but yet during our time of incarceration without the proper rehabilitation, we mentally could stay the same age we were upon entering prison? Also, if you don't gain the right tools, skills, or knowledge, then the odds are stacking against you even further. If you were not aware, you must evolve with time as it moves along and progresses and you must adapt to age-appropriate thinking, speaking, and actions. It is so easy to not realize that you aren't growing or elevating mentally in this setting because you're so caught up in the fact that you're doing real time in prison, or by the negativity that's going on around you. Many days, I sit back and analyze the men around me and I become upset because some of these men deserve to be in society, helping raise their children, helping their parents, the elderly and filling the many roles that we are absent from.

Another thing that is alarming is that many men in this environment live in the past or can't let the past go. What I mean by that is, its guys who constantly talk about things they did 20 or 30 years ago like that matters. I understand these are the memories that we have from our past and may not have much too talk about with a younger guy or someone that just left society so we should try our best to look towards the future and manifest things that we would like to accomplish. If you don't remain future focused in this setting, you can possibly get stuck in the past mentally. It's unfortunate that we have to evolve without having the proper experiences in certain areas of our lives, due to being imprisoned so long. They say experience is the best teacher but what if you haven't experienced certain things, situations, responsibilities, or adulthood yet? My only true personal advice is to learn from seeing and hearing other people's failure and success. This is a method to stay up to speed on reality and keep yourself grounded on what's ahead of you in the future. When you are thinking and operating from a logical and realistic standpoint, you will be prepared for the things that you have yet to encounter or experience in your future.

In conclusion for whomever may be reading this book, especially if you're young, black, or incarcerated, better yourself, change your mentality, make smarter decisions and choices. Also put yourself in the best positions possible! Finally, when good opportunities present themselves take full advantage of them!

Acknowledgements

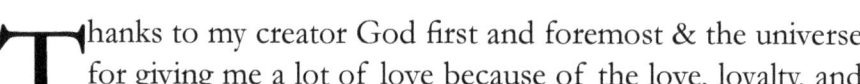

Thanks to my creator God first and foremost & the universe for giving me a lot of love because of the love, loyalty, and goodness, I put out into it.

Thanks to my grandfather Henry Rigsby (R.I.P.) And My mother Ms. Ann for being my biggest supporters in life...

Thanks to my Sisters Carrie and Bianca for always being there. Thanks to My cousin Tay Tay for coming through when I be needing you the most. Lil Steve you my brother til the end! I love you Aria Baer & Brielle Lacy(My Daughters), Even Though I wasnt privileged to see y'all throughout my bid or be there for yall . Shout Out to my King, Stowes , and Powell family, I love all Y'all.

R.I.P -Dwight Stowes , Adam Cade, 84th Dre, Lenard Pinson, Beverly Thomas, Wayne Stowes, Dominique "DC" Walker" And Many more loved ones of mines & The ones that lost their lives too early on...

Thanks to the certain brothers from my hood (84th -Superior, Decker Wadepark,)who stayed in my corner regardless of false rumors that were said about my character and didn't let the time or distance tear our brotherhood down. We are brothers since day one and that bond can't be broken... Jay, Bo, Cnell , Yao, And Rico. Jay I'm so proud of you for leaving prison and creating success in everything you do. And for the ones who left me for dead, I still got love for y'all.

Finally, too everyone that is incarcerated, keep striving to get your freedom back soon as possible and don't let nobody or nothing stop you from doing so! Being in prison has shown me who truly cares about me and shows who loves me, even when I have nothing to offer but conversation. Going through this struggle has fueled me and motivated me to want better out of life.

#Instagram- (FreeAntonioStowes)
#Future Focu$ed
#Free Us Out The Struggle
#Its way more to life

Fatherless Fathers

Fatherless Fathers Is The Start Of A Cycle , A Cycle That Is So Deep Rooted In Are Past And Are History...

So Many Wonder Is This Really A Mystery ...

Who Knows How Are Lives Would Of Turned Out If We Had A True Father Figure, Ones That Could Guide Us And Show Us How To Use Are Gifts That Was God Given...

Missing That Biological Connection That Is So Needed And Very Relevant...

Incarcerated Fathers, Prematurely Dead Fathers And Fathers That Are Physically Free But Non Existent ...

We All See What's Going On But Don't Nobody Wanna Listen , Its A Shame Because Are Kids Are Gonna Continue Too Miss Us ...

So Many Single Mothers You Can't Tell Me This Not An Issue , They Claim To Understand But They Don't Know What We Been Thru ...

I Feel For All The Fathers Who Wish They Could Do What They Had Too Do , Unfortunately They Got Us In The Penitentiaries Stuck Like Glue ...

So We Gotta Break The Bad Habits, So We Can Live Up To Are Full Potential...

Lead By Example Fathers , Make An Impact On Are Sons And Daughters, Who Are So Lost Without Us ...

My Hurt and Pain
By Antonio Stowes (Buckey Lo) 2019

My Hurt And Pain Leaves Me In Shock...
My Hurt And Pain Makes Me Feel Like, IMA Always Be Left Out And Forgot About...
So Many Days And Nights In The Cell You Can't Tell Me This Anit Hell...
And They Always Told Us If You Don't Straighten Up You'll Surely Fail...
Now All I Can Do Is Hope And Pray For Some Mail ,Whether Its On Jpay Or Snail Mail...
Life And Time Passing Me By , I Feel Like About Time I Go Home Cars Will Actually Fly...
So Many Tears My Eyes Are Dry , And Every Time Im On The Phone I'm Wondering Who Gone Lie...,
These Are The Reasons Why We Try Too Stay High...
No Telling What The Future Will Bring...
And They Wonder Why We Have So Much Mental And Emotional Pain...
But At The End Of The Day, Its All For Somebody Else Financial Gain, ...
And For Anybody Who Is Ever Been Incarcerated I Know You Feel My Pain,...
Missing Years And Years Out My Life Should Never Be A Game, All For Street Fame But Soon As You're Down Bad You Gone Be

Considered A Lame... ,

   You Never Could Of Told Me At This Point In My Life I'll Be On The Verge Of Going Insane, And All Are Mothers Can Do Is Shake Their Heads In Shame... ,

   And Its Way Much More To The Story Of My Hurt And Pain ...

www.ingramcontent.com/pod-product-compliance
Ingram Content Group UK Ltd.
Pitfield, Milton Keynes, MK11 3LW, UK
UKHW022218230426
12048UKWH00016BA/918